Co

. . . .

Introduction 5

Law firms do not exist in a vacuum 11

What does business excellence look like? 17

What if business excellence is absent? 39

The path to business excellence for your firm 61

The world for law firms in 2012 73

2012: will you make it a year of success
for your firm? 81

Further reading 87

About the authors 91

GAINING COMPETITIVE EDGE

UNPRECEDENTED

....

IN A CHANGING LEGAL MARKET

LIAM WALL
NICOLE BACHMANN
ANDREW HALL

Copyright ©2012 Liam Wall, Nicole Bachmann, Andrew Hall
Published in 2012 by SRA Books

This book has been produced for Bear Space LLP
Bear Space LLP
59 Lambeth Walk
London SE11 6DX
www.bsllp.co.uk

A CIP record for this book is available from the British Library.

ISBN 978-0-9567553-3-9

Designed, produced and published by Sue Richardson Associates
SRA Books
Sue Richardson Associates
Minerva Mill Innovation Centre
Station Road
Alcester
Warwickshire B49 5ET
T: 01789 761345
suerichardson.co.uk

Printed and bound in Great Britain by TJ International, Padstow

GAINING COMPETITIVE EDGE

UNPRECEDENTED

IN A CHANGING LEGAL MARKET

. . . .

Introduction

. . . .

Introduction

This is a book for anyone who has started the job of managing partner with the question: 'Well, how difficult can it be?' and then found out exactly how difficult it is. This is a book for those who can see other firms around them with partner profits reaching six or seven figures while their own lag well behind. This is a book for those who believe that profit would be obtainable if only the rest of the firm would do what they are told. Especially, this is a book for those who wonder why some people are so convinced that 2012, with the arrival of alternative business structures (ABSs) and outcomes-focused regulation (OFR) will be the end of the world as we know it.

Over the last decade, Bear Space has consulted with legal partnerships that operate in 19 countries and collectively comprise nearly 600 partners, with annual revenues of £500 million.

In our experience, legal partnerships face the same core challenges as all businesses.

These challenges include how to:

- ▶ find and retain the right people
- ▶ find and retain the right customers
- ▶ keep growing
- ▶ create an environment of motivation throughout the firm
- ▶ make a profit for the owners.

This book draws on our extensive knowledge of law firms and business to set out how those challenges will be thrown into sharp relief by the introduction of the ABS and OFR regimes. It offers a course of action that will enable you to advance your firm and boost your competitiveness, regardless of how you perceive the threat from ABS competitors. Following the suggestions in this book will put you in a position where your firm has nothing to fear from OFR.

Whatever the new market environment brings for law firms over the next few years, we strongly believe those firms that embrace it and take considered action will succeed. The firms that carry on as if nothing has changed will, over time, wither and die.

As the managing partner, will you be the one to future-proof your firm?

GAINING COMPETITIVE EDGE

UNPRECEDENTED

....

IN A CHANGING LEGAL MARKET

....

Law firms do not exist in a vacuum

....

Law firms do not exist in a vacuum

The Law Society was formed in 1825 and received its first Royal Charter in 1831. The foundation of some of today's firms predates either of those events. The cumulative knowledge of how to run a firm has therefore been developed and preserved over a long period of time.

Perhaps it is inevitable for a profession that is necessarily involved in the application of precedents, and where years of experience or years on a lockstep are still commonly used to measure commercial worth, to simply perpetuate a way of doing things – including the understanding of how to lead a successful legal practice.

The link between partners and the ministrations of the Law Society has been singularly successful in producing a legal profession in the UK that is technically innovative and proficient in the provision of legal advice. Whether that link has been equally successful in equipping firms to be thriving commercial enterprises in an environment where the parameters are suddenly shifting – and at pace – is less certain.

The introduction of OFR provides firms with a greater degree of flexibility in how they operate and places the achievement of the right outcomes for clients, rather than compliance, firmly at the centre of regulation. The SRA's guidance makes clear that OFR is designed to empower firms to implement the right systems and controls to achieve those outcomes. Consequently there is a need to exercise greater judgement to deliver on this responsibility.

If your firm is recognised for providing a good service to clients and your people are able to readily adapt to the new regulatory framework then you should be in a good position to take advantage of the increased flexibility of operation that OFR affords.

These changes place much greater importance on the need for firms to become outstanding commercial entities, while retaining their tradition of technical excellence. This leaves you with the challenge of gaining competitive advantage in a rapidly changing market place, readying itself for the entry of new competitors in the form of ABSs.

To meet all these challenges your firm needs to become excellent in business.

GAINING COMPETITIVE EDGE

UNPRECEDENTED

IN A CHANGING LEGAL MARKET

· · · ·

What does business excellence look like?

· · · ·

· · · ·

What does business excellence look like?

· · · ·

In simple terms, 'business excellence' means being excellent in the three core disciplines of business activity – people, operations and finance (the key characteristics of which are illustrated in Figure 1 on page 20).

It also means maintaining an enterprise that is healthy and able to respond dynamically to the constantly changing commercial environment in which it operates. The health attributes (illustrated in Figure 3 on page 68) of an organisation able to deliver on excellence comprise: empathy, followership, leadership, confidence, innovation, capability, competence and rigour.

The key to health and flexibility is found in the internal alignment of all business activities, the quality of execution throughout the organisation and an external focus that utilises what is happening in the broader business environment to its advantage. This leads to the healthiest organisations being able to adapt to changing circumstances better than the competition.

Figure 1: Business excellence achieved

Empathy — Followership — Leadership — Confidence

Innovation — Capability — Competence — Rigour

People

Finance

Operations

Fully engaged & motivated teams

Highly valued stakeholder relationships

Absolute focus on delivering client value

Pervasive culture of responsibility

Proactive communication & collaboration

Optimal business growth

Effective use of capital

Consistently good profitability

Optimal client profitability ratio

Key financial drivers understood by all business leaders

Highly effective structures & processes

Consistent performance results

Exceptional sales & marketing operation

Effective performance measures & targets

Clarity & consistency of purpose

Achievement of both excellence and health is a major challenge. A lot of businesses struggle to excel in even one or two facets. Leaders are so steeped in the day-to-day running of their business, focusing only on the short term, that they fail to take sufficient time to contemplate tomorrow's market needs.

The primary driver for commercial success is found in a deep-seated quality of leadership across the business, coupled with confidence in the business model and growth strategy. These foster engagement of all staff, engendering capability, flexibility and competence across the organisation.

Organisations that master those qualities and pair them with a strong desire/commitment to innovate, become the exemplars for outstanding client experience and typically progress to be the most admired and successful businesses.

Once people, operations and finance integrate seamlessly and the leadership places equal priority on the health of the organisation, a business has the ability to continuously instigate change, rather than cope with it after it has happened.

In this section, we provide an explanation of the attributes of people, operations and finance excellence shown in Figure 1. For each attribute, we provide a brief real-life example, taken from our work with many businesses and law firms over the last decade.

Absolute focus on delivering client value: everything anyone in the firm does is motivated by delivering value to the client, listening to the client's needs and wants first and then tailoring the service offering accordingly.

An IT maintenance company on a continuous drive to improve customer service did a client survey to establish whether what they thought their customers bought was what their customers really bought.

They found out that their clients were not buying 'IT maintenance', but 'sleeping at night' and 'absence of hassle'. The company realigned both communication and client service towards that result, which led to a doubling of turnover within a year, increased client satisfaction, referrals and new client attraction.

Fully engaged and motivated teams: everyone pulls together and all team members are able and willing to put team objectives above their own.

An equity partner in a large law firm was seeking ways to attract new commercial business that would stay with the firm over the long term. He identified the entrepreneurial community as a likely source, as well as an untapped market for high-quality legal advice.

He gained commitment from his equity partners to take this strategy forward and to create a cross-department and cross-function entrepreneurs' group, with both senior and junior partners stepping forward to be involved. Within three months, they created a product offering in collaboration across functions, which helped them develop that market. They also increased their marketing effort in this area through collaboration with other external organisations.

The products increased the firm's attractiveness to the target market – the entrepreneurial community – and resulted in new instructions from them. They also caught the eye of investors in that community, which has led to further new business for the firm.

Highly valued stakeholder relationships: clients, suppliers and staff feel valued and heard and their contributions are acknowledged.

The managing director of a drinks company ensured that his staff knew how much he valued their contribution by practising 'leadership by walking around'. This gave his staff the opportunity to discuss issues directly with him and created an environment for them to step forward with ideas and contributions.

A line supervisor came forward with an idea on how to reorganise his production line to reduce water consumption. The managing director requested a written proposal, which the supervisor provided with help of his line manager. The case was approved and tested on one line, with the result that water consumption was reduced by more than 50%.

»

The solution was then rolled out to other plants, which led to substantial cost-savings for the company. The supervisor received recognition in both financial and leadership terms, which enhanced the culture of engagement, innovation and pride in the business. This culture has led to many more improvements, cost savings and new opportunities for the company.

Pervasive culture of responsibility: everyone in the firm is clear about what is expected of them and, in turn, expects to be held accountable for what they deliver.

At a large professional services firm, every member of staff was always conscious of the need to do the best possible job, with the support of their peers. This led to a continuous dialogue between functions with the view to improving behaviours, service and results. Mistakes were discovered and dealt with early, performance was monitored by team members as well as leaders and people were willing to stay late to assist a colleague in finding a solution to a specific problem or work out a new opportunity. The escalation of problems

»

was expected and supported. 'Finger pointing' rarely arose. In consequence, the firm obtained a reputation for excellence with their customers and suppliers that helped them achieve their targets year on year.

In a large record company, the engagement of staff was such that any member of the team who picked up a phone would take immediate ownership of the issue raised by the caller and see it through to completion, no matter what department was 'responsible' for that issue or activity. The person taking the call would take responsibility for having the matter resolved – with the help of whichever other member of staff they needed. Everyone would pull together and no one ever said, 'Not my problem, you have to speak to X'. As a result, the record company remained ahead of the competition in service delivery and client satisfaction, which led to a continuous flow of new business.

Proactive communication and collaboration: everyone is willing to step forward with ideas, take responsibility for the way they communicate and take the initiative to find solutions together.

The head of department in a law firm was planning ahead and realised that workloads were likely to decline due to the credit crunch. He took immediate action to inform staff of this and explained to the team that the future looked bleak if they, as a firm, did not find a solution to the situation.

One of the assistants was determined to do what she could to limit the impact of the downturn. With the partners' approval, she joined a local networking group and through it introduced a good level of new work to the team. As other colleagues followed her example, the firm's fee earning was not impacted by the downturn to the extent of most firms.

Operations

Exceptional sales and marketing operation: the target market(s), the way to reach them and how to engage and build relationships with prospects and clients is clearly defined; the firm has a clear sales process built on understanding the needs and wants of the identified market(s) and enough people who can close sales to ensure a consistent client acquisition and retention rate.

A business-to-business marketing agency, on a continuous drive to improve profits and client flow, went through an assessment of their marketing and sales processes and found some room for improvement. Their research established that their unique identifiers were:

a. their direct and no-nonsense approach to identifying the problems in their prospects' and clients' marketing strategies

b. their focus on doubling the business of their clients, rather than creating award-winning campaigns.

They used this new understanding to redefine the market they should target for business.

This helps them to gain clarity about the business they want to be and have and encourages them to say no to anything (including potential clients) that doesn't get them there.

They have undertaken more extensive research of this new market in order to better target their marketing expenditure to generate new leads. Once their marketing operation brings in the leads, their

»

sales process is also completely aligned with their unique identifiers.

They use the Sandler sales method, which is geared towards weeding out prospects who are not a good match. Once they sign up clients, they continually maintain the relationship, with excellent after-sales service that checks for further needs and wants, with the constant mind-set of 'how can we help?'. This leads to proactive cross-selling of all departments and has resulted in a continuous flow of new business with consequent growth of turnover and profits.

Clarity and consistency of purpose: everyone in the firm is clear about the firm's vision, mission and goals. All staff operate to a common standard and their efforts are focused unfailingly on the overall success of the business.

A client at one firm instructed a corporate partner on a company matter. The corporate partner recognised the need for input from an assistant and arranged a meeting for the client with the assistant. After the completion of the matter, the client telephoned to speak to the corporate assistant and **»** was surprised to find they were actually a member of the litigation team. Two teams, two distinct types of advice and one client experience.

As a result, the client increased the number of instructions to other teams in the firm and became an advocate of the firm's services.

Highly effective structures and processes: organisational structure and processes enable the firm to operate under changing conditions in a consistent manner and deliver against key performance indicators (KPIs) in the right order of priority.

In a medium-sized law firm, the partners and all staff have a good awareness of the key drivers of the business and relative priorities. As a consequence, they budget at less than 90% of capacity to allow flexibility in deployment of resources.

Therefore, if a major client assignment demands significant additional resource, they are able to provide it without any significant disruptive impact on the rest of the firm and other clients. Although some might argue the firm's approach is wasteful, in reality it has enabled flexibility and a higher level of service quality for clients – attributes that have won them valuable additional business.

Effective performance measures: ensuring that performance of all staff and resources is reported in relevant terms to ensure a consistent level of performance. This process, usually referred to as KPI reporting, focuses on value creation for clients and not just financial data.

In reviewing their performance, a firm realised that focusing their attention solely on fee-earning targets was no longer sufficient due to falling demand. They introduced an additional target for fee earners to identify a set number of potential clients or referrers each month, with whom they would develop strong relationships. In addition, they were targeted on the quality of the relationships with their existing clients, measured by the number of referrals and testimonials given.

This change in performance measures refocused the fee earners on the appropriate actions and is resulting in renewed growth of the business.

Consistent performance results: the individuals, departments, functions and business units deliver against performance goals and targets over the short, medium and long term, through cascading goals and targets and aligning them throughout the organisation.

A large professional services firm operates a very structured process, whereby the top level goals of the business are rolled down through the whole hierarchy. The head of each fee-earning team is expected to put the relevant targets in place. These are validated with their senior executive to ensure alignment with the overall strategy, goals and targets of the firm.

Effective performance measures are in place to ensure results are managed and monitored, which enables appropriate remuneration according to results. KPIs include people development/mentoring, contribution to cross-departmental forums and external industry groups, in addition to financial performance and client satisfaction metrics.

This firm is consistently at, or near, the top of peer group ratings in terms of growth, profitability, standing as an employer and client satisfaction.

Finance

Optimal client profitability ratio: consistently obtaining a return on each client that ensures 100% client satisfaction, an acceptable financial return for the firm and the best possible return on client acquisition cost.

A firm routinely profiled client profitability. It found time and again that the most profitable clients were able to provide a thorough instruction, were realistic concerning timescales and paid bills on time and at the rates agreed. This understanding was built into the client engagement process and used to train fee-earning staff so they could more effectively respond to and monitor clients' behaviour.

The result was that profitable clients received a good level of service in line with the profit that they were generating for the firm. Profits at the firm were significantly increased and sustained. This also improved client perception of the firm's quality of service as fee earner time and energy focused on satisfying realistic client expectations.

Consistently good profitability: year on year delivery of profits that are sufficient to support ongoing investment in the future of the business.

A firm, keen to maximise the benefits of its success to support continued growth, committed to a rolling three year business plan from which future investment decisions (capital expenditure, new offices, staff progression and recruitment) were set. This approach immediately introduced a clear link that everyone understood, between profitability growth and the development aspirations of the firm. In particular, it broke the historic attitude of many, who saw profitability of the firm as being only in the interest of the partners.

This also meant contentious decisions made in previous years (like the marketing budget and new partner appointments) were now more readily approved by partners. The result was consistent year on year fee growth with a high level of partner consensus.

Optimal business growth: developing and implementing growth plans that reflect the strategy of the firm and that are affordable in terms of finance, skills and resources.

From client feedback a firm identified an opportunity to expand a fee-earning team by 85% over the following 12 months. In the past, when faced with such opportunities, the firm would recruit new staff ahead of the expected increase in demand regardless of the impact on cash flow and partner profits.

As a result of their new business planning process, which included financial performance and affordability targets, this was no longer an option. The firm chose to deploy two partners, from a team that was under-utilised, for business development of the new service and used locums to perform the initial pieces of work they secured.

This enabled the market opportunity to be validated with minimal impact on cash flow. The opportunity they had identified was successfully established, the firm expanded the team with minimal risk within the available cash flow and increased billings were achieved.

Effective use of capital: ensuring that the firm delivers an acceptable level of return on capital employed (RoCE).

The marketing director of an international firm advocated the purchase of new customer relationship management (CRM) software. This represented a significant investment for the firm and would replace an existing software product.

The proposed new CRM system would integrate with other software systems at the firm and, consequently, enable analysis of client billing data alongside client matters. It would also enable the various relationships that the firm had internationally with its corporate clients to be more easily understood by a wider range of people, thereby enabling more cross-selling opportunities between teams and offices.

The finance team supported the marketing director in preparing the internal business case, which projected the new system would enable an increase in fee income of at least 15% from their top 100 corporate clients. The project was approved with a return on general partnership capital of 25%.

Key financial drivers understood by all business leaders: educating all leaders on the key financial metrics of the firm and ensuring that their personal KPIs are linked to those metrics.

> When looking at ways to improve billing, a large firm noticed that most of the discounts offered by the firm were on small bills. It became apparent that approximately 5% of the total billing was regularly written off against individual bills of less than £1,000.
>
> The firm communicated this during the partner's conference and continued to communicate the point with monthly reports on this type of discount. By highlighting this KPI and reminding partners of its importance and impact, the firm achieved, over time, a significant reduction in such discounts and, consequently, ongoing improvements in billings.

From the preceding descriptions and examples we hope you will have developed an understanding of the attributes of business excellence and what they do for organisations that apply them. You might also have gained some ideas on how they complement the technical excellence that you seek to deliver.

If you are interested in assessing the level of business excellence currently displayed by your firm, please complete our initial assessment of excellence online at **http://tiny.cc/InitialBEA**

To broaden your understanding of the consequences of the absence of business excellence, read on.

GAINING COMPETITIVE EDGE
UNPRECEDENTED
· · · ·
IN A CHANGING LEGAL MARKET

· · · ·

What if business excellence is absent?

· · · ·

• • • •

What if business excellence is absent?

• • • •

If excellence is missing from your business, you will undoubtedly experience some or all of the following:

▶ Difficulties in winning and retaining clients.

▶ An inability to recruit and/or retain high-calibre staff.

▶ Disruptive and/or inconsistent behaviours between personnel across the firm.

▶ A pervasive sense that the firm is struggling for business.

▶ Habitual discounting of fees in order to get invoices paid.

▶ Profitability under increasing pressure.

▶ Partner earnings declining.

▶ Banking conditions becoming less favourable, which may have a negative impact on cash flow.

▶ Policies and procedures being set but not followed.

▶ A general sense that the organisation lacks leadership and direction.

▶ Seemingly simple decisions deferred indefinitely.

Figure 2: Lack of business excellence

Doubt

Indolence

Abdication

Malfunction

Dissociation

Ineptitude

Indifference

Stagnation

Unwillingness to take responsibility

Internal communications not functioning

Constrained business growth

Poor return on capital

Limited understanding of financial implications

Weak cost controls

Lack of client centricity

People

Finance

Poor client profitability ratio

Disengagement of teams

Dysfunctional relationships with stakeholders

Operations

Business does not deliver expected performance

Ineffective/inadequate sales & marketing operation

Failure to deliver outcomes on time and to budget

Lack of clear roles and responsibilities

Dysfunctional interfaces between functions and/or teams

All of these are serious danger signs that may ultimately lead to shrinking of the firm, a take-over or (in the worst case) liquidation.

Add to this the impact of the ABS legislation becoming effective in 2012 and you have a heady cocktail of challenges for the managing partner – or any partner – of a law firm.

How do you recognise a lack of business excellence? The key characteristics are illustrated in Figure 2 on page 42.

In the following section, we illustrate the attributes of an organisation in which excellence is absent from the people, operations and finance disciplines of the firm.

For each of the attributes of absence of excellence we, again, provide an explanation, followed by a brief real-life example. Do not be surprised if some of these are familiar, as they occur in most businesses at some time.

People

Lack of client centricity: people are inwardly focused and more concerned with what they provide, rather than what the client wants/needs; unwillingness to take responsibility for client issues.

A partner at a firm insisted that his clients meet him each quarter for a review of matters generally. The partner often cancelled the meetings at short notice if other client matters required his urgent attention. When the meetings were held the partner used them primarily as an opportunity to pitch services from other departments of the firm.

Over time, one major client felt increasingly that the meetings were not for his benefit. He subsequently refused to attend further meetings and ultimately moved to another firm.

Dysfunctional stakeholder relationships: 'the left hand doesn't know what the right hand is doing' – people work in silos seeking solutions in isolation, which leads to loss in human capital, synergies and effectiveness.

In a large law firm with multiple teams there was much talk about cross-selling and referring clients from one team to another. Despite the talk, the level of referral was very low. Partners in team A felt their clients would not be treated properly by team B in terms of service, technical solutions or pricing.

The outcome of this dysfunction was reduced billing and profit for the firm, a lack of continuity in the provision of legal services for their clients and lost opportunities to create client loyalty. Not only did the firm fail to maximise revenues from existing clients, but they continuously struggled to find enough new clients.

Unwillingness to take responsibility: people take a step back to avoid being held accountable for their performance whenever a new initiative is launched or an important decision is needed.

A few years ago, we were asked to discuss an important financial matter with a law firm. We met the managing partner, the finance partner and a third equity partner. The managing partner presented the problem, the finance partner contradicted the managing partner, while the third equity partner took a completely different position from his peers.

The managing partner sought the agreement of two of his partners to solve a specific problem but was not prepared to risk taking the decision on his own. At an important moment for the firm, none of the senior partners was willing to take responsibility for solving the problem and making the necessary decisions.

This is only one example of the behaviours of these partners. Although this firm continues to trade, profits are weak and the rate of growth is significantly behind that of its competitors.

Disengagement of teams: people don't feel heard or appreciated, which leads to them refusing to get involved and (in the worst case) sabotaging progress.

A new support manager wanted to impress the managing partner with his team's performance. Without discussion with the team, the manager introduced a rule that all requests made before 3pm would be dealt with on the same day. The team duly nodded when the rule was announced but the actual responsiveness was unchanged, with many requests remaining unanswered after two days.

The unresponsive approach of the team emanated from the old and substandard equipment they had to work with. Constant equipment failures meant it was impossible to meet the deadline. The new manager had not thought to discuss with his team why they were 'unresponsive' or get their perspective.

The manager's autocratic approach resulted in the team failing to report the equipment deficiencies either as an existing problem, or as an obstacle to the implementation of his new rule. Not surprisingly, this manager failed to deliver a high-performing team.

Internal communication not functioning: a mind-set of 'information is power', i.e. people neither share knowledge and experience nor request help when they need it, creates a fertile ground for misinformation, misunderstandings and rumours.

A successful partner was appointed as the new managing partner in a firm. He was a dominant and forceful character. He had observed previous managing partners leading from the front and noted that they always seemed to have the answers to everything. He concluded, therefore, that he should exhibit the same behaviour.

He quickly issued new policies and guidelines without consultation or input from others at the firm. Management meetings were changed from monthly to quarterly – to save time. The managing partner worked hard on the administration of the firm, which meant he rarely left his office. He invested none of his time in communicating with the members of the firm, obtaining their views or explaining why he was making changes.

The lack of a proper explanation for changes resulted in rumour and speculation about the managing partner's motives and his remoteness from the rest of the firm. A rumour took hold that the firm was being prepared for a merger that would lead to widespread redundancies.

This resulted in one of the better performing teams leaving for another firm of their choice rather than be merged with an (as yet) unknown entity. None of the speculation was accurate but the consequence of the managing partner's lack of communication and engagement was the loss of some key people and reduced fee income for the firm.

Operations

Ineffective/inadequate sales and marketing operation: there is no structured approach to identify prospective clients and campaign to win their business; marketing effort on business development is non-existent or fails to deliver adequate results; lack of measurement of the effectiveness of both sales and marketing efforts.

A firm decided to invest in marketing in order to win new clients. They believed all they needed to do was communicate their technical expertise and prospective clients would naturally come to them. »

They purchased a new CRM system to increase the frequency of their marketing communications to clients and prospects. Consequently, potential clients heard a good deal more about the technical strengths of the practice.

However, their message was not addressed at what clients felt was important and did not increase the personal dialogue between partners and their clients. It did nothing to increase new instructions. In fact, it had a negative effect on the image of the firm, because, due to the lack of relevance of the message to them, many potential clients thought they were victims of a spam attack.

Business does not deliver expected profit margins: forecast profit margins eroded by ineffective use of resources and inattention to results, delivery and measurement of KPIs.

Based on their view about their fee rates, bookable hours and cost base, a firm produced a budget, forecasting a profit margin of 40%. The key metric by which the firm monitored performance was the number of hours recorded by each fee earner.

»

However, they failed to hold fee earners responsible for delivering the hours that had been budgeted and did not take action in respect of consistently poor performers.

Furthermore, they did not monitor costs, resource allocation, achievement of new client instructions and client satisfaction. Consequently, they were unable to see their true progress towards achieving their forecast, which resulted in the firm consistently under performing against budget.

Their level of performance was below average for a firm of this size and, therefore, impacted the firm's ability to attract new partners, pay staff at a market rate and invest in their infrastructure.

Failure to deliver outcomes on time: the structure and processes of the firm don't operate effectively, which leads to missed deadlines and/or non-completion of activities.

A firm's standard terms of engagement required payment within 30 days. Each fee earner and their respective head of department were required to monitor and manage outstanding debts. They each had online access to the relevant internal systems and also received regular standard debt reports for their areas of business. Senior fee earners received a bonus related to achieving a certain level of collections as well as billing. In addition, the firm employed two credit controllers.

Despite these support mechanisms and performance metrics, in excess of 50% of the debt ledger was more than six months old at any time. Although the credit controllers were permitted to send out statements on overdue accounts, they were not allowed to escalate the need for payment with a firm letter, because heads of departments were concerned about damaging client relationships. For the same reason, they even extended credit on new matters to clients who had a history of failing to pay their bills.

As a consequence, the firm had a significant overdraft, which was expensive to maintain. The firm continued with a high exposure to bad debts/ default and poor cash flow.

Lack of clear roles and responsibilities: people are confused about their KPIs, job description and what is within/without the scope of their role and influence.

A 10-year qualified fee earner had been at his current firm for three years. He was recognised as diligent, trustworthy and hard working. When he joined the firm, it had been made clear there was the potential for him to make partner. However, at that time no one explained to him what the criteria for awarding partnership were.

At appraisal, the fee earner asked if he was on target for partnership. The head of department informed him that he would not be made a partner because his billing performance was well short of the required target and had been since the fee earner joined the firm, he did not have a client following and he had failed to introduce any new clients to the firm.

So after three years of anticipation, the fee earner discovered he had to effectively start from scratch, striving to achieve these criteria. He was deeply disappointed at this prospect and decided to leave the firm.

The failure of the head of department to ensure that the fee earner understood the criteria for making partner, from the start, caused the firm to lose a valuable fee earner (and potential partner) as well as the investment they had made in him.

Dysfunctional interfaces between functions and/or teams: any formal processes exist only within departments and there is no holistic view of the operation of the firm; people operate in silos, leading to abdication of responsibility for the overall result at the point of handover to another department or team.

To communicate more effectively with their clients, a fee-earning department within a firm decided to establish a database of client contact details. This was done on a spreadsheet, maintained within the department.

Unknown to the fee-earning department, the marketing team was already performing the same task using an appropriate CRM system. However, the marketing team did not make this information available to other departments.

》》

Consequently, the clients of the fee-earning department were invited to a function at the firm twice – both by the fee-earning department and the marketing team. This did not present the professional image sought by the firm and was extremely wasteful of time and effort by the respective teams.

Finance

Poor client profitability ratio: low and/or inconsistent return on client acquisition cost due to a lack of understanding of client needs and wants; disproportionate amount of time/resource deployed on clients who are poor value to the firm; a lack of cross-selling of all services the firm can provide; failure to monitor the true financial value of each client to the firm and adjust the firm's response accordingly.

Many firms assess client value by reference to the size of the client's billing without taking into account the costs of servicing the client.

One firm gave their largest client a 15% reduction in all fee rates, provided free seminars and access to research facilities as well as extended payment terms. These actions were taken on a piecemeal basis with the commendable intention of encouraging client loyalty and increased instructions. In reality, these incentives were provided at the expense of all other clients of the firm.

A focus on client profitability would have revealed the largest client was loss-making for the firm. In addition, by giving so much to one client, the firm stifled its ability to win more profitable work elsewhere.

Constrained business growth: falling profits leading to reduced cash flow make it increasingly difficult to effectively fund critical business growth activities, such as marketing and business development.

When a small firm experienced a reduction in turnover it began to suffer weak cash flow. The initial reaction of the partners was that they and the senior managers each needed to devote more time to winning new instructions, in order to recover the lost revenue. After some months, they realised that their individual efforts were not delivering the level **»** of new business the firm needed. In addition, they were finding it difficult to devote sufficient time to business development alongside their client work.

They had little understanding of how marketing stimulated new client introductions, as this was not measured by the firm. Consequently, during the budget process they followed the guidance of their accountant and reduced all 'overhead' spend, which resulted in the marketing budget being cut by four-fifths.

By reducing the firm's marketing budget and failing to understand how effective marketing generates opportunities, the partners prolonged the weak cash flow position and the firm continued to suffer reduced fee income.

Weak cost controls: expenditure not controlled against a budget that reflects forecast revenues, leading to poor financial performance.

Many underperforming firms set their expenditure budget first and then work out the fees needed to deliver an acceptable profit for the partners. This approach assumes that overhead is fixed when it **»** is in fact variable and that all overhead is valuable when in fact it is only valuable if it contributes to profit.

Using this traditional approach, a firm set a budget that maintained the ratio between fee earners and secretaries. Over a period of years, the volume and acceptance of email (and Blackberry usage) by clients and fee earners meant that the demand for traditional secretarial duties had roughly halved.

By failing to reduce the number of secretaries in line with the operational needs of the firm, the firm experienced reduced profits over several years.

Poor return on capital: the effectiveness of capital expenditure is not formally monitored; lack of process to enable appropriate prioritisation and selection of options for investment.

A firm engaged in an office refurbishment programme nine months into the credit crunch when fee income had started to slide. On completion of the refurbishment, the firm had smarter offices. However, 20% of the offices were now vacant due to staff reductions, arising from falling demand for their services.

In addition, they had an outstanding loan for the refurbishment from the bank, on which the repayments were taking an increasingly larger slice of their profits, as fee income continued to fall.

It had taken two years for the original plans to receive approval from the planning authorities and the partners took the view that they just wanted to see the job finished. A formal assessment of the situation, based on a robust business case rather than 'gut instinct', would most likely have led them to a different and less costly solution.

Limited understanding of financial implications: everyone relies on the 'finance partner' to know if the financial performance of the firm is on track; senior staff lack sufficient appreciation of how their actions impact financial returns.

At an international firm, the finance director calculated for each team whether the profit of the team was in surplus or deficit compared to the profits paid to the partners in the team. His objective was to establish whether the performance of the teams was sufficient to fund their respective partner's earnings. The finance director proposed to the partner group that the results of his calculations should be used to determine the allocation of the firm's bonus pool to individual partners. One partner strongly argued that teams in deficit should be axed.

This partner was not financially astute and had not been paying proper attention to the financial performance of his own team. When the firm implemented the new measures, the partner in question discovered to his shock that his team's bonus allocation was zero, because they were in deficit.

Having spent time looking at business excellence and the consequences of its lack, you might be interested in assessing where your firm is on the spectrum of excellence. To do so, you can undertake our initial assessment of excellence online at **http://tiny.cc/InitialBEA** On completion of the assessment, you will receive a brief evaluation report by email.

GAINING COMPETITIVE EDGE

UNPRECEDENTED

IN A CHANGING LEGAL MARKET

· · · ·

The path to business excellence for your firm

· · · ·

The path to business excellence for your firm

Welcome back. How did you do? Unless you are excellent in all aspects, you will probably now ask yourself what changes you need to make to improve.

Before you embark on the path to improvement, we suggest you give some thought to how change is undertaken in your firm and what the likely barriers are to it happening.

Consider the following questions:

1. **How does your firm take decisions?**

2. **What steps do you take to identify what is needed (other than doing our initial assessment of excellence)?**

3. **How do you ensure that the requisite changes are widely understood and adopted/ implemented effectively?**

1. How does your firm take decisions?

▶ Do you, as the managing partner, have the trust and authority of your equity partners to run the firm as you see fit – with their active support and backing?

▶ Are you playing 'decision by committee', where you arrive at conclusions, rather than make decisions; where each partner is more interested in his/her agenda and department, than the firm as a whole; where what the equity partners say and do are not always congruent…?

▶ Are you having difficulties managing the contributions of the equity partners, because each of them feels they can do as they please and only occasionally, with luck, do you arrive at a consensus?

2. What steps do you take to identify what is needed (other than doing our initial assessment of excellence)?

▶ Do you continually assess how effective your people, processes and systems are?

▶ Do you know the competitive position of your firm in the changing market place?

▶ Are you consistently winning new business?

▶ Is the financial performance of the firm continually improving?

3. How do you ensure that the requisite changes are widely understood and adopted/ implemented effectively?

▶ Do you plan the implementation of change, taking into account **RACE** (who is **R**esponsible, who is **A**ccountable to whom, who needs to be **C**ommunicated with, how do you **E**ngage them)?

▶ Do you understand the impact of your firm's culture on the change?

▶ Are you taking steps to analyse whether you have to adapt that culture to enable the change?

Depending on your answers to these questions, you will face few or many barriers to implementing change in your firm. The ability of your firm to overcome any barriers and implement change effectively is a function of its organisational health.

If you remember, right at the introduction to business excellence we asserted that it is the healthiest organisations that are better able to adapt to changing circumstances than the competition. The health of an organisation is reflected in the vital signs of internal alignment, quality of execution and external focus. If you have completed our initial assessment of excellence, you will already have an indication of the relative health of your firm.

Figure 3 on page 68 illustrates the health attributes of an organisation able to deliver on excellence.

Consider where your firm is on the scale of 1 to 10 for each attribute. If you want to capture your scores and receive some feedback on their meaning, please go to **http://tiny.cc/OrgHealth.**

Figure 3: Business health attributes

Abdication	The extent to which leaders inspire actions by others and provide a clear sense of direction	Leadership
Dissociation	The degree of enthusiasm that drives employees to put in extraordinary efforts to deliver results	Followership
Indifference	The extent to which staff feel heard and understood and make an effort to understand their colleagues	Empathy
Doubt	The certainty and conviction with which employees perform their role and engage with stakeholders	Confidence
Stagnation	The quality and flow of new ideas and the organisation's ability to adapt as needed	Innovation
Malfunction	The scale of the collective skills and talent present to execute strategy and create competitive advantage	Capability
Ineptitude	The ability of all individuals to perform their role in a self directed manner	Competence
Indolence	The discipline to evaluate performance and risk in a structured and consistent way across the organisation	Rigour

1 ... 10

If you have scored at least 8 across all of these attributes, your firm is showing all the characteristics of a healthy organisation, so your path to business excellence should be an exciting and enjoyable journey.

If you score your firm below 8 on:

▶ Leadership, followership and competence – **internal alignment** is likely to be elusive

Without internal alignment, it is unlikely you will achieve shared objectives that are supported by your firm's culture and at the same time are meaningful to individual employees. Without shared objectives, the energy and effort your people put into their work is likely to dissipate productivity and results, rather than contributing to them. Consequently, you will find it difficult to achieve sustained competitive advantage.

▶ Leadership, innovation, empathy and confidence – **external focus** will be weak or lacking

Weakness in external focus will negatively impact the quality of your firm's engagement with customers, suppliers, partners and other external stakeholders. Poor engagement with any of them will severely hamper your ability to tailor your current and future offerings to your market, which in turn will inhibit your firm's continued growth.

▶ Leadership, followership, competence, confidence, capability and rigour – **quality of execution** will be an issue

Poor quality of execution will result in unnecessary levels of re-work and poor delivery, leading to low levels of client satisfaction, which will impact the firm's reputation. A poor reputation will lead to difficulties in winning and retaining clients with a consequent impact on recruiting and retaining the right talent.

If left unaddressed, the lack of any of these attributes will make your travel towards an excellent business much more unsettled: you will find more and steeper barriers to overcome, which will slow you down and prevent the momentum created by a well-planned change programme. This is likely to severely jeopardise the results you can achieve.

Having read this far and completed our initial assessment of excellence, you will either be clear about what you intend to do next, or you will want some further understanding and guidance.

If the latter is true, take our comprehensive business excellence assessment online at:
http://tiny.cc/IndepthBEA

Following completion of the assessment, you will receive a report showing the areas of relative strength and weakness and suggesting some initial actions to address them.

This report will provide a good basis for you to get started, or, if you prefer, to have a conversation with an experienced advisor who can support you in getting your firm on the path to business excellence and your long term competitive edge.

GAINING COMPETITIVE EDGE

UNPRECEDENTED

••••

IN A CHANGING LEGAL MARKET

••••

The world for law firms in 2012

••••

The world for law firms in 2012

As we have already noted, law firms do not exist in a vacuum. Therefore, it is important to understand the external context for the changes you will now be contemplating and the likely impact of market conditions on your way forward.

There are many uncertainties surrounding law firms in 2012.

The UK economy

The UK economy is in poor health following the downturn precipitated by the financial crisis in 2007–2008 and the more recent developments in the Eurozone. Most commentators and economists agree that it is also very uncertain when good health will be restored. Business confidence is elusive and growth remains patchy in many sectors. Public spending will remain constrained for the current parliament and further tax increases are still to have an impact. Whatever the timing of any changes in the status quo, this represents a very challenging environment for business.

Law firm funding

At a time when firms are facing increased operating costs, their ability to fund cost increases has been significantly reduced. The banks, faced with the weak balance sheets of their law firm clients (and in some cases their own), have been reappraising the risk profile they assign to law firms. This has reduced the availability of credit for many firms and is penalising firms that have poor credit control processes or that are doing work under extended credit terms. It is unlikely the banks will revise this lending position any time soon.

Mergers

Many firms suffering from lower volumes of work, a drop in profit and a lack of available credit have sought salvation through merger. By rationalising their support functions, these merged firms have improved profitability in the short term.

However, the resulting merged firms have inherited many of the operational problems that led them to seek a merger in the first place. In addition, in mergers made out of necessity, the likelihood that the two cultures will be synergistic is very low.

Consequently, there is low probability that the merger of two law firms (where at least one party is already financially weak) will deliver a new, strong, commercially-viable enterprise.

Outcomes-focused regulation (OFR)

The SRA is fundamentally changing the relationship with those that it regulates. The new approach to authorisation, supervision and enforcement will be risk based, proportionate, targeted, more open and constructive.

This provides opportunity and challenge to firms in equal measure. More control and greater flexibility will result in an easier relationship with the regulator for those firms that manage their business effectively. They will be able to concentrate on taking advantage of market opportunities, which will create a smoother path towards gaining competitive advantage and growing their firm.

Those firms that struggle to operate as a successful commercial enterprise will feel both the increased pressure to achieve mandatory outcomes and the heat of the competition.

Alternative business structures (ABS)

Historically, the provision of legal services has never been of interest to the owners of other commercial enterprises, because of the requirement for UK law firms to be under the control of solicitors. Consequently, the only competitive pressures have come from other law firms, all operating with similar capital structures and similar desires for high profits for all partners.

The advent of ABS provides for a fundamental change in the basis of ownership and, hence, the opportunity for businesses and entrepreneurs with no previous interest in the provision of legal services to own and manage law firms.

The size of the legal market, currently estimated at £23bn with the top 100 firms accounting for £15.5bn, together with perceptions of high margins and high-value services, will attract new entrants from other sectors of commerce to become active owners of UK law firms. It is inevitable, therefore, that the competitive threat will increase for the majority of UK firms.

The top 100

The partners in the top 100 firms expect to achieve ongoing profit growth and that means some level of continued growth in fees. Where is that growth going to come from when they already account for nearly 70% of the UK market?

The answer is, from the 9,900 firms outside the top 100. If you don't believe that new entrants to the market via ABS will make life hard, consider the very real threat posed by the leading firms coming after your clients and even your staff.

Also, consider what the top 100 firms could achieve if, with their strong balance sheets, they had easy access to funds from external sources in the same way that a plc does.

Where does this leave your firm and you as managing partner?

The next few years are likely to be a period of intense competition and innovation within the legal market. New organisations will offer legal services in new ways. "Tesco law" has become a metaphor for commoditisation, i.e. high volume, low value work. However, what if it really means reasonable value work available 24 hours a day 7 days a week, with free parking and with premium branded products?

How many of your core client matters are already

coming under competitive threat from commoditised and new offerings delivered by some of your competitors?

How many of your partners and staff would find it easy to adapt to that new competitive environment? Which of them would be keen to join a firm that is more dynamic and able to provide them with opportunities to grow?

What does this mean for your firm?

As the managing partner, what are you intending to do about it?

GAINING COMPETITIVE EDGE

UNPRECEDENTED

....

IN A CHANGING LEGAL MARKET

....

2012: will you make it a year of success for your firm?

....

2012: will you make it a year of success for your firm?

••••

You may view the changes outlined here as a massive headache – or a major opportunity – for the future of your firm.

Managing partners who anticipate only headaches and choose to ignore the changes impacting on the legal market will, in our opinion, leave themselves and their firms badly exposed to the whims of an increasingly competitive and commercially aggressive environment.

Managing partners who recognise the opportunity to lead their organisation into a profitable and exciting future and take on the mantel of building an excellent business, will set themselves up for successfully creating a firm that attracts the best talent and clients.

You are uniquely positioned to take the lead in your firm. You can choose to build a strong partner consensus and implement an active management culture. You can ensure that your clients are firmly at the heart of every aspect of the firm and that your people service the needs of those clients with creativity and vigour.

By embracing this approach, you will be well equipped to move rapidly up the scale of business excellence, thereby giving your firm a clear and sustainable competitive advantage.

To help you to decide on your next steps, we invite you to complete our comprehensive business excellence assessment online at
http://tiny.cc/IndepthBE

Following completion of the assessment, you will receive a report showing the areas of relative strength and weakness and suggesting some initial actions to address them.

If you decide that you need an effective programme of change, you will require a thorough analysis taking into account views from a broad representation of people in your firm – ideally conducted by an impartial third party.

»

For an initial consultation on how to go about this, get in touch with us online at **http://www.bsllp. co.uk** or telephone 020 7735 6623.

Whichever way you decide to go forward, enjoy future-proofing your firm and continually striving for excellence – both technically and as a commercial enterprise.

If you do, you can expect to lead a healthy and successful firm that is and will remain ahead of the competition, because it continues to respond effectively to market conditions – whatever they may be.

GAINING COMPETITIVE EDGE

UNPRECEDENTED

. . . .

IN A CHANGING LEGAL MARKET

. . . .

Further reading

. . . .

Further reading

Beyond Performance: How great organisations build ultimate competitive advantage by Scott Keller and Colin Price, John Wiley & Sons Inc: New Jersey, 2011

The Future of Management by Gary Hamel, Harvard Business School Press: Boston, 2007

The Fifth Discipline: The art and practice of the learning organization by Peter M Senge, Random House: New York, 1993

Good to Great by Jim Collins, Random House: London, 2001

The Leadership Challenge: How to keep getting extraordinary things done in organizations by James M Kouzes and Barry Z Posner, Jossey-Bass: San Francisco, 1995

The Five Dysfunctions of a Team: A leadership fable by Patrick Lencioni (J-B Lencioni Series), Jossey-Bass: San Francisco, 2002

GAINING COMPETITIVE EDGE
UNPRECEDENTED
IN A CHANGING LEGAL MARKET

. . . .

About the authors

. . . .

About the authors

• • • •

Liam Wall is a chartered accountant and the founder and managing partner of Bear Space LLP. He is highly regarded by the CEOs and managing partners with whom he works for his lateral thinking and the clarity he brings to commercial and organisational issues. An experienced finance executive, Liam is atypical in his practical, pragmatic approach to business solutions.

Since 2001 Liam has consulted extensively within the legal market but has also worked with firms in the IT, distribution, food manufacturing, professional practice, retail and not-for-profit sectors. Prior to 2001 Liam was a financial controller, UK finance controller, group financial controller and finance director for four diverse, successful and rapidly changing companies.

Liam is a co-author of *BusinessWise*, and Chair of Trustees for a London based charity.

Nicole Bachmann is a founding partner, with Andrew Hall, of Haywood Mann and founder of Brook & Mann, experts in entrepreneurial leadership. She is also the co-founder of www.beatprocrastination.com

Nicole undertakes leadership and performance development engagements in four languages for a variety of organisations across Europe. She has designed and delivered a wide range of tailored programmes to tackle operational effectiveness, performance and productivity issues. In addition Nicole coaches executives and entrepreneurs in effective business communications and leadership.

Nicole holds a Masters degree in Law from the Paris Lodron University, Salzburg, and she is a visiting lecturer for the Business and Management Training Centre at the University of Essex Business School.

Nicole is a Fellow of the Institute for Independent Business International, a founding member of the International Association of Coaches and a patron of Entrepreneurs World. She is the author of *Speaking Volumes* and co-author of *BusinessWise.*

Andrew Hall is a founding partner, with Nicole Bachmann, of Haywood Mann. He is an advisor and mentor to owners and entrepreneurs in a broad range of businesses, a patron of a London-based collaboration network for entrepreneurs and an associate of a City venture capital firm.

Andrew has been the managing director of a UK IT systems and consulting business and an associate partner in the world's leading management and technology consulting organisation. Andrew's work has included engagements with several organisations responsible for aspects of the UK legal system, such as the Home Office, the Ministry of Justice and the former Lord Chancellor's Department, as well a variety of law firms and other professional practices.

Andrew has developed many successful teams and individuals through his personal leadership and management in a number of international organisations throughout a corporate career spanning over 30 years.

Bear Space specialises in providing professional financial management and accountancy services to law firms. Their deep understanding of the nature and style of professional practices enables them to provide insightful and pragmatic guidance to partners on improvements to cash-flow, client profitability, forecasting and financial control. They are particularly skilled at analysing and improving the efficiency of processes and IT systems that support the financial function of a firm. They are also able to provide finance managers, up to and including Finance Director-level, on a part-time or interim basis. To find out more, contact Liam Wall on 020 7735 6623 or lw@bsllp.co.uk or visit www.bsllp.co.uk

Haywood Mann is a venture established to focus specifically on excellence in action. Its purpose is to help businesses gain competitive advantage by becoming healthy organisations that excel in the core disciplines of people, operations and finance. To find out more about Excellence in Action, contact Nicole or Andrew at www.haywoodmann.co.uk